# Wishing you
# 365 Days of Kindness
# 52 Weeks of Patience
# 12 Months of Love

**Rosa Linda Cruz Counseling & Wellness Services, LLC**
**Copyright 2024**
**ISBN: 9798323410200**

1st Edition: April 19, 2024

The author of this book does not dispense medical advice or prescribe the use of any technique as a form of treatment for physical, emotional, or medical problems without the advice of a physician, either directly or indirectly. The intent of the author is to offer information of a general nature to assist in the journey of well being.

# Super Hero Students

# Wellness Strategies
for You

## by
## Rosa Linda Cruz
## LPC-S, Author & Consultant

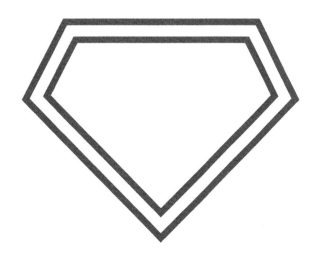

A special thank you to my grandchildren, students and community members who continually ask for fun, engaging and interactive workbooks. My grandchildren are a source of energy and remind me to be present & live a life filled with joy, awe and wonder. My students and community members inspire me to be a life learner and to continually share mental health strategies within our communities. Your support and encouragement are sincerely appreciated and hope that you will find this resource helpful in your life journey.

# This book belongs to

SUPER HERO NAME:_____

_____

# How have you been feeling the last 2 weeks?

**What are emotions?**

Emotions are something that we feel inside ourselves. Emotions are temporary visitors and they keep changing. There are different kinds of emotions that we experience. Sometimes we feel happy, sad, angry, scared, worried and so much more.

"Students who can understand and manage their emotions are more likely to:
- express emotions by speaking calmly or in appropriate ways
- bounce back after feeling strong emotions like disappointment, frustration or excitement
- control impulses
- behave appropriately – that is, in ways that don't hurt other people, things or themselves.

And this is good for students because it helps them learn, make friends, become independent and more."

# How have you been feeling the last 2 weeks?

(match the emotion to the emoji)

sleepy

scared

angry

sad

love

happy

confused

silly

# SUD  Subjective Units of Distress

Let us begin today and assess how you have been feeling the last 2 weeks. Let's rate your stress level. I always like to give everyone a few options so choose one from the following:

Circle stress level within the last 2 weeks:

**1 bit of stress**       **5 some stress**       **10 extremely stressful**

3

# SUD  Subjective Units of Distress

Let us begin today and assess how you have been feeling the last 2 weeks. Let's rate your stress level. I always like to give everyone a few options so choose one from the following:

Circle stress level within the last 2 weeks:

**1 bit of stress**              **5 some stress**                **10 extremely stressful**

# Window of Tolerance

purple minion vs. yellow minion

all closed doors vs. some closed doors vs. all doors open
no access vs. off-line vs. on-line

false alarm vs. real alarm

# Window of Tolerance

<u>WINDOW of TOLERANCE</u>

Flexible   Open   Curious   Present   Safe   Capable   Mindful   Engaged
Connected   Self soothing   Able to self regulate   Learn   Listen
*ON-LINE*
*YELLOW MINION*
*ALL DOORS OPEN*

<u>HYPERAROUSAL</u>

Anxiety   Anger   Aggression   Rage   Fight   Flight   Hypervigilance   Panic
Overwhelmed   Rapid Breathing   Physical tension   Thoughts racing   Out of control
*OFF-LINE*
*PURPLE MINION*
*SOME DOORS CLOSED*

<u>HYPOAROUSAL</u>

Passive   Shutdown   Numb   Freeze   Fatigue   Shame   Exhaustion   Unfocused
Tired   Sleepy   Unmotivated   Slow moving   Helpless   Too scared to move
*NO ACCESS*
*POSSUM*
*ALL DOORS CLOSED*

6

# Getting to know You

**GET ENOUGH SLEEP**

What time do you go to sleep at night?_____

**DRINKING WATER**

How many glasses of water do you have everyday?_____

**EATING HEALTHY FOOD**

What is your favorite fruit?_____

What is your favorite vegetable?_____

What is your favorite food?_____

**SURROUND YOURSELF WITH LOVED ONES**

Who loves you the most?_____

_____

Why do they love you so much?_____

_____

Why do you love them so much?_____

_____

Who are your friend(s)?_____

_____

What do you like about your friends?_____

_____

Why do your friend(s) like you?_____

_____

# Getting to know You

My favorite color is _____

My favorite holiday is _____

My favorite animal is _____

My favorite movie is _____

My favorite tv show is _____

School is _____

Right now, I feel _____

I like to _____

My family is _____

I worry about _____

I want to be _____

I am afraid of _____

I have fun when _____

I love _____

# Getting Started

**Neutral   Bland**

**Thoughts**

**Facts & Evidence**

**Emotions**

**Body Sensations**

**Behaviors**

# Getting Started

Pause

Breathe

Notice, Observe & Non-Judgmental


Neutral Space


Event (look at the facts, evidence, data and patterns of behavior)


New Thoughts

New Emotions

New Body Sensations

New Behaviors

# Examples

**PAUSE**
**BREATHE**
**NOTICE, OBSERVE & NON-JUDGMENTAL**


**NEUTRAL SPACE**


**EVENT** *Example*
*My parents grounded me.*


**THOUGHTS** (no facts, no evidence, no data and no patterns of behavior)
*Before Example*
*I will be grounded forever. My life is over. It's not fair.*

**FEELINGS**
*Before Example*
*angry, sad and worried*

**BODY SENSATIONS**
*Before Example*
*tense, heart beating fast and head hurts*

**BEHAVIORS**
*Before Example*
*stomping my feet, making faces, and yelling at everyone*

# Examples

**PAUSE**
**BREATHE**
**NOTICE, OBSERVE & NON-JUDGMENTAL**


**NEUTRAL SPACE**


**EVENT**
*Example*
*My parents grounded me.*


**NEW THOUGHTS (facts, evidence, data and patterns of behavior)**
*After Example*
*I did not do my chores. I failed my math class. I stayed up late talking on the phone.*
*My parents give me an allowance when I do chores.*
*I always pass my math class when I do my homework.*
*My parents let me use the phone all day until 8pm so I can get a good night's sleep.*


**NEW FEELINGS**
*After Example*
*calm and confident*


**NEW BODY SENSATIONS**
*After Example*
*capable and clear headed*


**BEHAVIORS**
*After Example*
*I am going to say I am sorry. I will start to do my chores again.*
*I will study and go to tutorial. I will stop using my phone late at night.*

# PAUSE and BREATHE

**1st Step**

**PAUSE**

This gives you time and space to go to the next step

**2nd Step**

**BREATHE**

You can use this strategy or other strategies.
You get to choose.  You need to practice everyday.
This will help your mind, heart and body to remember
what you are trying to do.

**3rd Step**

**NOTICE, OBSERVE & NON-JUDGMENTAL**

Take time to notice these temporary feelings.  Are they
trying to tell you something? Is this a false alarm or a real
alarm?  Be Non-Judgmental.  Practice kindness, patience
and love for yourself.

# PAUSE and BREATHE

**1st Step**
**PAUSE**

**2nd Step**
**BREATHE**

**3rd Step**
**NOTICE, OBSERVE & NON-JUDGMENTAL**

# CHAIR YOGA

Let's get started with this stretching exercise.

Gently move your head to the right side and hold for a few seconds.
Center your head.
Gently move your head to the left side and hold for a few seconds. (Repeat 4x)
Take a deep breath in and take a deep breath out.

Gently roll your shoulders back on a count of of eight.
Gently roll your shoulders forward on a count of eight.
Take a deep breath in and take a deep breath out.

Gently wiggle your fingers and stretch arms outward as if reaching for something.
Gently bring your arms back in and wiggle your fingers. (Repeat 4x)
Take a deep breath in and take a deep breath out.

Gently rotate your wrists outward on a count of eight.
Gently rotate your wrists inward on a count of eight.
Take a deep breath in and take a deep breath out.

Gently turn your torso to the right and hold for a few seconds.
Center your torso.
Gently turn your torso to the left and hold for a few seconds. (Repeat 4x)
Take a deep breath in and take a deep breath out.

Raise both legs and point toes outward and hold for a few seconds.
Keep both legs up and point toes inward and hold for a few seconds. (Repeat 4x)
Take a deep breath in and take a deep breath out. (Repeat 4x)

# CHAIR YOGA

**Benefits:**

**Decreases stress**
**Builds strength**
**Feelings of well being**
**Allows for refocus and concentration**

**Reflection:**

**When is a good time to practice, apply and implement this exercise in your daily routine?**

**What kind of feelings do you get after this exercise?**

**Where do you feel them in your body?**

**What are your thoughts after this exercise?**

**How will this help you in your daily life?**

# BREATHE

Let's get started with a simple breathing exercise.

Place one hand on your chest and the other hand on your tummy.
Place your feet to the ground.
Listen to your breath.
Focus on the inhale and exhale.
Inhale deeply and hold for a few seconds.
Exhale deeply.
Repeat 8x

Practice kindness, patience and love for yourself.
Just notice, observe and be non-judgmental.

# BREATHE

**Benefits:**

**Increases energy**
**Reduces tension**
**Increases feelings of calm and well being**
**Relaxes**

**Reflection:**

**When is a good time to practice, apply and implement this exercise in your daily routine?**

**What kind of feelings do you get after this exercise?**

**Where do you feel them in your body?**

**What are your thoughts after this exercise?**

**How will this help you in your daily life?**

# BREATHE

Here are some additional fun bonus breathing techniques for all ages.

**Shoulder Breath Roll**
take a deep breath in while pulling shoulders up towards the ears
then
take a deep breath out while dropping the shoulders back

**Taco Breath**
curl the edges of your tongue together like a taco
take a deep breath in through the taco
hold the breath for a few seconds
then gently breathe out through the nose

**Bumble Bee Breath**
breathe in deeply and slowly keeping mouth closed
make a humming noise while breathing out

**Reflection:**

When is a good time to practice, apply and implement breathing techniques in your daily routine?

What kind of feelings do you get after this exercise?

Where do you feel it in your body?

What are your thoughts after this exercise?

How will this help you in your daily life?

# BREATHE

Here are some additional fun bonus breathing techniques for all ages.

Volcano Breath
pretend hands and arms are like lava flowing from a volcano
start with hands in front of the heart with palms touching
keeping hands together reach straight up and breathe in
separate hands and move arms down to the side of your body and breathe out

Dragon Breath
interlace fingers under the chin
breathe in and raise elbows as high as possible
breathe out and lower elbows back down

Hot Air Balloon Breath
cup hands around the mouth and breathe in deeply
and
while breathing out expand hands outward as if blowing up a great hot air balloon

Reflection:

When is a good time to practice, apply and implement breathing techniques in your daily routine?

What kind of feelings do you get after this exercise?

Where do you feel it in your body?

What are your thoughts after this exercise?

How will this help you in your daily life?

# BREATHE

**Lady Bug Breath Activity**

# BREATHE

This is a favorite among many students.

**Lady Bug Breath**

**Reflection:**

When is a good time to practice, apply and implement breathing techniques in your daily routine?

What kind of feelings do you get after this exercise?

Where do you feel it in your body?

What are your thoughts after this exercise?

How will this help you in your daily life?

# RANDOM ACTS OF KINDNESS

Random Act Activity

Encourage someone

Write a thank you note

Volunteer

Take time to listen to a friend

Write a positive note on a post it and place it on someone's desk

Be grateful

Speak kindly

Give a genuine compliment

Hold a foodbank drive

Surprise someone with a treat

Do a chore without being asked

Smile at someone new

Send a gratitude email

# RANDOM ACTS OF KINDNESS

**Benefits:**

**Generates good feelings**
**Positive mood**
**Increases connection with others**
**Creates emotional warmth**

**Reflection:**

**When is a good time to practice, apply and implement random acts of kindness in your daily routine?**

**What kind of feelings do you get after this exercise?**

**Where do you feel it in your body?**

**What are your thoughts after this exercise?**

**How will this help you in your daily life?**

# RANDOM ACTS OF KINDNESS

**Draw a picture of you doing a random act of kindness.**

# RANDOM ACTS OF KINDNESS

Write about something you did that was a random act of kindness.

# MUSIC

**Music Activity**

**Write about or draw your favorite songs and singers. How does the music make you feel?**

**I would gently encourage you to incorporate music in your morning routine. If possible, implement it throughout your day as background music. Playing your favorite songs to finalize the evening has many benefits. This is also a great transition tool that can be implemented when you go from one environment to another. You may even want to add a little singing and dancing.**

# MUSIC

**Benefits:**

**Increases energy**
**Elevates mood**
**Boosts your concentration and focus**
**Strengthens learning and memory**

**Reflection:**

**When is a good time to practice, apply and implement music in your daily routine?**

**What kind of feelings do you get after this exercise?**

**Where do you feel it in your body?**

**What are your thoughts after this exercise?**

**How will this help you in your daily life?**

# MUSIC

**Music Activity**

**Write about or draw your favorite songs and singers. How does the music make you feel?**

# MUSIC

**Music Activity**

**Write about or draw your favorite songs and singers. How does the music make you feel?**

# Journaling

Research still supports journaling as a way to process thoughts and feelings on daily events, past memories, challenges and daily moments of gratefulness. This can consist of writing, making lists, drawing, sketching or coloring.

Keep it simple
Be creative
Write a poem about it
Create a comic strip on the events
Make a song
Color your feelings
Create a new narrative

# Journaling

**Benefits:**

**Improves communication skills**
**Allows time to review thoughts**
**Focuses on positive life moments**
**Releases and processes emotions**

**Reflection:**

When is a good time to practice, apply and implement journaling in your daily routine?

What kind of feelings do you get after this exercise?

Where do you feel it in your body?

What are your thoughts after this exercise?

How will this help you in your daily life?

# Journaling

**Write a story or draw your favorite memory.**

# Journaling

Write a story or draw your favorite memory.

# Sunshine Corner

Grounding ourselves means taking a moment to pause, place feet on the ground and be present. Take a moment to incorporate your senses which include sight, smell, hear, taste and touch. I gently encourage you to take time to surround yourself with items that bring calm, inner joy and incorporate visual, auditory, olfactory, gustatory and tactile sensations to your environment.

# Sunshine Corner

**Grounding activity**

**List everything you see.**

**List everything you hear.**

**List everything you smell.**

**List everything you taste.**

**List everything you touch.**

# Sunshine Corner

**Grounding activity**

**List everything you see.**

**List everything you hear.**

**List everything you smell.**

**List everything you taste.**

**List everything you touch.**

# Sunshine Corner

**Benefits:**

**Encourages calmness**
**Reduces stress**
**Elevates mood**
**Feels centered, strong and solid**

**Reflection:**

**When is a good time to practice, apply and implement grounding in your daily routine?**

**What kind of feelings do you get after this exercise?**

**Where do you feel it in your body?**

**What are your thoughts after this exercise?**

**How will this help you in your daily life?**

# Laughter Yoga

**List or draw things that make you happy.**

**"Your brain does not know the difference between genuine and fake laughter."**
Ha Ha Ha Ha Ha Ha Ha Ha Ha Ha Ha Ha Ha Ha Ha Ha Ha Ha Ha Ha
He He He He He He He He He He He He He He He He He He He He
Ho Ho Ho Ho Ho Ho Ho Ho Ho Ho Ho Ho Ho Ho Ho Ho Ho Ho Ho Ho

# Laughter Yoga

**Benefits:**

**Improves mood**
**Gives more energy**
**Increases happy feelings**
**Adds joy in your life**

**Reflection:**

When is a good time to practice, apply and implement laughter in your daily routine?

What kind of feelings do you get after this exercise?

Where do you feel it in your body?

What are your thoughts after this exercise?

How will this help you in your daily life?

40

# Bonus Strategy
## Write or draw your happy place here
(see, hear, smell, touch, and taste)

Reflection:

What kind of feelings do you get after this exercise?

Where do you feel them in your body?

What are your thoughts after this exercise?

How will this help you in your daily life?

# Bonus Strategy
## Write or draw your happy place here
### (see, hear, smell, touch, and taste)

**Reflection:**

**What kind of feelings do you get after this exercise?**

**Where do you feel them in your body?**

**What are your thoughts after this exercise?**

**How will this help you in your daily life?**

# Gentle Reminders

Additional Strategies to add in your daily life.

Exercise
Yoga
Paint
Garden
Music
Meditation
Dance
Color
Sing
Walk
Nature
Crochet
Surf
Read
Sketch
Play
Bubbles
Hobby
Prayer
Volunteer
Laugh
Journaling
Grounding
Earthing
Breathing techniques
Talk to a trusted adult

# Gentle Reminders

**List of extra strategies I would like to add to my daily life.**

# What I learned today

45

# What I learned today

# My favorite techniques

# My favorite techniques

# Other tools I can use

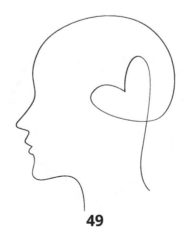

# Other tools I can use

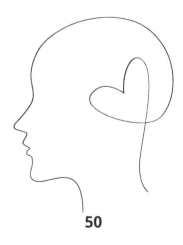

# I can talk to_____
## when I am out of my window of tolerance

# I can talk to_____
## when I am out of my window of tolerance

# Learning techniques are important because

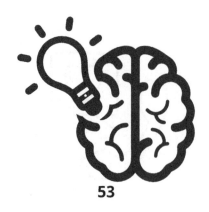

# Learning techniques are important because

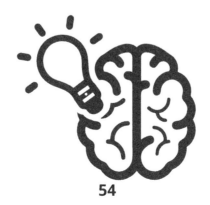

# Words to describe emotions

| Happy | Angry | Sad | Fearful |
|---|---|---|---|
| proud | mad | lonely | scared |
| peaceful | bitter | hurt | anxious |
| curious | let down | isolated | insecure |
| joyful | disappointed | grief | weak |
| free | frustrated | ashamed | helpless |
| valued | awful | empty | frightened |
| loving | annoyed | disappointed | overwhelmed |
| optimistic | jealous | embarrassed | worried |
| playful | betrayed | hurt | inferior |
| interested | hostile | guilty | nervous |
| trusting | furious | despair | excluded |
| accepted | humiliated | vulnerable | worthless |
| thankful | skeptical | depressed | inadequate |
| grateful | provoked | remorseful | threatened |

# Words to describe body sensations

| <u>Ugh</u> | <u>Oooh</u> | <u>Won't stay still</u> | <u>Ouch</u> |
|---|---|---|---|
| heavy | tense | buzzy | bruised |
| dense | tight | shaky | achy |
| blocked | hot | jumpy | sore |
| cold | sweaty | pulsing | nauseous |
| hollow | burning | bubbly | raw |
| numb | explosive | jittery | tender |
| empty | heart pounding | energized | hurting |
| dull | out of breath | twitchy | inflamed |
| exhausted | wobbly | antsy | itchy |
| drained | light headed | fidgety | swollen |
| blurry | dizzy | on edge | puffy |

# Bonus Activity: Emotions
## How are they feeling? Color the matching emotion.

| | | |
|---|---|---|
| Happy | Sad | Anxious |
| Calm | Worried | Happy |
| Love | Bored | Happy |
| Angry | Sad | Confused |
| Happy | Sad | Angry |

# Bonus Activity: Emotions Word Search
## Find the words hidden in the puzzle.

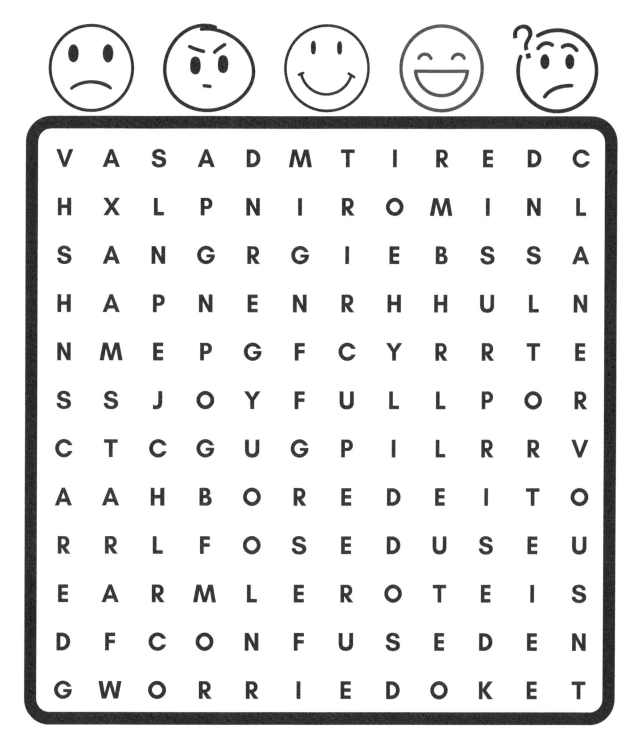

```
V  A  S  A  D  M  T  I  R  E  D  C
H  X  L  P  N  I  R  O  M  I  N  L
S  A  N  G  R  G  I  E  B  S  S  A
H  A  P  N  E  N  R  H  H  U  L  N
N  M  E  P  G  F  C  Y  R  R  T  E
S  S  J  O  Y  F  U  L  L  P  O  R
C  T  C  G  U  G  P  I  L  R  R  V
A  A  H  B  O  R  E  D  E  I  T  O
R  R  L  F  O  S  E  D  U  S  E  U
E  A  R  M  L  E  R  O  T  E  I  S
D  F  C  O  N  F  U  S  E  D  E  N
G  W  O  R  R  I  E  D  O  K  E  T
```

| | | | |
|---|---|---|---|
| BORED | JOYFUL | CONFUSED | SAD |
| ANGRY | SCARED | SURPRISED | CALM |
| HAPPY | WORRIED | NERVOUS | TIRED |

**Bonus Activity: Feelings Check-In**
**Right now, I'm Feeling ...**

**I feel this way because ...**

_____

_____

_____

_____

**Something that might help is ...**

# Bonus Activity: Express your feelings

Use the colors to express emoji emotions.
Remember, it's okay to feel all these emotions,
and coloring can help you understand them better.

| Emotion | Emotion Emoji | When do you feel like this? |
| --- | --- | --- |
| Happy (Yellow) | | |
| Sad (Blue) | | |
| Surprised (Purple) | | |
| Angry (Red) | | |
| Calm (Green) | | |

# BONUS STRATEGY: DRAW THE MOUTH FOR EACH ONE.

# BONUS STRATEGY: FEELINGS
## Draw your emotions on the events.

| | | |
|---|---|---|
| Your friend gets angry at you. | You have a new game. | You see a ghost. |
| You win first place. | You get grounded. | You forget your homework. |
| Your parent gives you money. | You watch funny movies. | Your tummy hurts. |

**BONUS STRATEGY: How Do I Feel?**

How do I feel when _____?

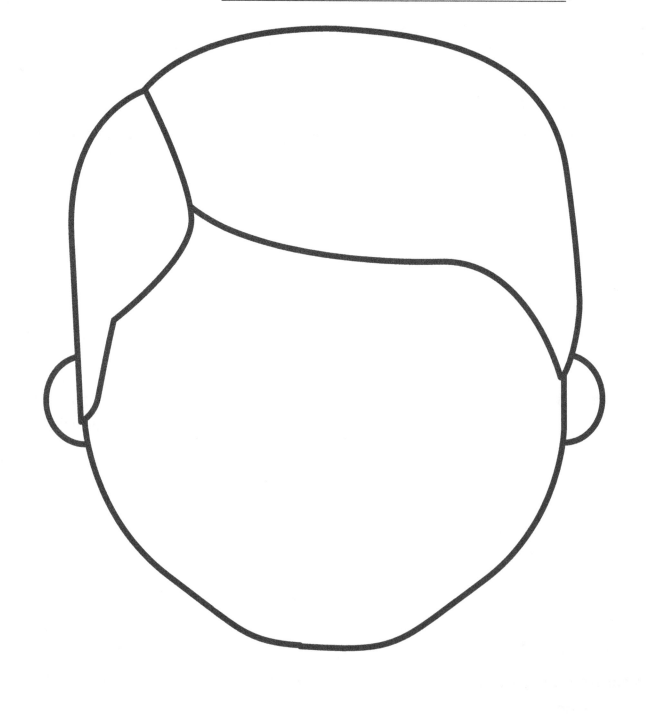

## BONUS STRATEGY: How Do I Feel?

**How do I feel when** _____ **?**

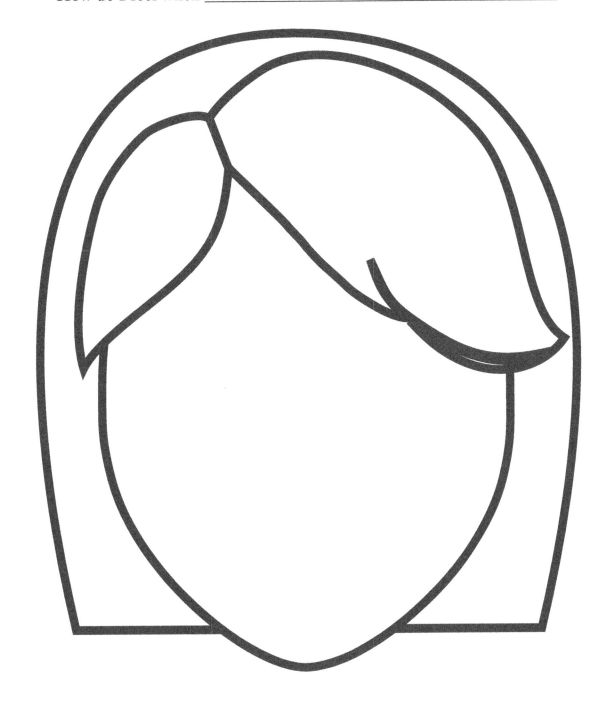

NOTES:

NOTES:

NOTES:

NOTES:

## Cited Resources:

https://tea.texas.gov/

https://greatergood.berkeley.edu/

https://traumaresearchfoundation.org/

https://grief.com/

https://happyfamilies.com.au/

https://www.laughteryoga.org/

https://www.sciencedirect.com/

https://www.calm.com/

https://positivepsychology.com/

https://psycnet.apa.org/home

https://drdansiegel.com/

https://feelingswheel.com/

Made in United States
Orlando, FL
08 May 2024